YOUR
NEXT
LEVEL
LIFE

YOUR
NEXT
LEVEL
LIFE

7 RULES OF POWER, CONFIDENCE, AND
OPPORTUNITY FOR BLACK WOMEN IN AMERICA

KAREN ARRINGTON

Mango Publishing
CORAL GABLES

Front Cover design by Joanna Price | joannapricedesign.com
Cover illustration: Jag_cz/Shutterstock
Layout & Design: Roberto Núñez

For permission requests, please contact the publisher at:
Mango Publishing Group
2850 S Douglas Road, 2nd Floor
Coral Gables, FL 33134 USA
info@mango.bz

For special orders, quantity sales, course adoptions and corporate sales,
please email the publisher at sales@mango.bz. For trade and wholesale
sales, please contact Ingram Publisher Services at customer.service@
ingramcontent.com or +1.800.509.4887.

Your Next Level Life: 7 Rules of Power, Confidence, and Opportunity for
Black Women in America

Library of Congress Cataloging-in-Publication number: #######
ISBN: (print) 978-1-64250-032-5, (ebook) 978-1-64250-031-8
BISAC category code: SOC010000, SOCIAL SCIENCE / Feminism &
Feminist Theory

Printed in the United States of America

Table of Contents

FOREWORD

The year was 1977 when I first met Karen at the University of Maryland, College Park. She and I had decided to pledge the sisterhood of Zeta Phi Beta that fall. She was line sister one and I was line sister two. When I tell you it was friendship-love at first sight, please believe me. We made an instant connection fueled by our wit, stubbornness, and insatiable sense of humor. You see, Karen was very comfortable with the pledge process as her older brother was a Phi Beta Sigma man and went to the same college. I, on the other hand, knew very little about how and why being a part of this sisterhood could go on to shape the rest of my life.

Karen was also the daughter of the mayor of Seat Pleasant, Maryland. She came from a prominent family where both of her parents were high achievers and expected the same from their children. As Karen's friend, I had no choice but to adopt those same high expectations and tried dearly to keep up with them. Truth be told, this was the foundation that carried me through to graduation when many of our freshman friends dropped out of college and went home early. Before either of us really could define what going to the "Next Level" meant, Karen was already taking me there.

Soon after graduation, Karen and I went in different directions. Her entrepreneurial route started with creating the Miss Black USA Pageant, an institution that is determined to, in Karen's words, help "Black women to claim their power, redefine their destinies, and defy expectations." Karen went on to create her own women's leadership coaching, consulting, and luxury travel company where she continues to teach, groom, inspire, and support all who come into contact with her passion and brilliance.

As for me, I was determined to kick down doors to the boardrooms of corporate America and started my professional career in the pharmaceutical industry. Twelve years there—followed by twenty-five years in tourism marketing—enabled me to do my Next Level work as an advocate, educator, mentor, and, more importantly, hiring vice president at one of the world's greatest family destinations on earth. This was my calling. Breaking into tourism as a Black woman executive was not without its obstacles—but the rewards, inroads and insights that I got to share with others made everything worthwhile.

After nearly thirty years had passed since Karen and I had last seen each other, I woke up one day and realized, *I could seriously use a vacation.* I needed to refuel my tank and spend time with my sisters. I booked Karen's Next Level Bali Retreat. I was hoping for a rejuvenating getaway, but I got so much more…

Before the trip even began, Karen and I reconnected by phone, and we talked forever and ever about everything that had happened since our college days and all that we had been through. Next came the long-ass plane ride to Indonesia (long, but so worth it!) and then a week of tropical bliss. Karen and I kept staring at each other in disbelief. In some ways, it felt like centuries since our last meeting. In other ways, it felt like barely a minute had passed.

Throughout that retreat, we shared our thoughts, constitutions, wit, senses of humor, willpower, words of wisdom, and joy of life with each other. We connected and reconfirmed that we can always go to another level in how deeply we care, share, and motivate. It was really overwhelming at times to be halfway around the world with my dear friend—riding elephants, eating Balinese food, praying in temples, fighting off monkeys, and worshipping in the sun. We both were in total agreement that you cannot give enough, because giving with a pure intention always comes back threefold.

There are many different definitions and ways to get to the Next Level in life, love, business, and relationships. You are well on your way by reading this book. Karen is beautiful, unassuming, highly intelligent, and well-traveled; she is absolutely the best person to take us all to the Next Level. She has already influenced my life in so many ways. Now it's your turn to receive some of Karen's visionary magic.

Enjoy this book. Read closely. Take notes. Let Karen take you by the hand and lead you into possibilities you hadn't even considered for yourself. Know that everything is possible. And, wherever you are right now, know that there is always room to grow, to rise, to step into that Next Level Life. There is always another level…and now it's time to find yours.

—Sheryl Taylor, vice president of Visit Orlando

INTRODUCTION

My name is Karen Arrington. I was born three years before Dr. Martin Luther King, Jr., delivered his "I Have a Dream" speech from the steps of the Lincoln Memorial. I was there—a little girl with chubby toddler cheeks, standing next to my parents—while Dr. King spoke those historic words.

I was too young to fully grasp the immensity of what was happening that day. But, on some level, I know it impacted me. The words sank into my bones. Seeds were planted. Because, for as long as I can remember, I have dreamed of a better world—a world of opportunity and limitless possibility.

At age fifteen, I led a protest to change the name of my middle school. Several years later, the county school board approved a petition to change the name from Roger B. Taney Jr. High School to Thurgood Marshall Middle School.

A few years later, as a college student, I found my voice in the literary pages of works about African American sheroes like Sojourner Truth and Harriet Tubman. Their stories ignited a spark that I couldn't rid myself of—to be a voice for the silenced, disenfranchised, and unheard women of color.

As I read aloud Sojourner Truth's Anti-Slavery Speech "Ain't I a Woman"—delivered in 1851 at the Women's Convention in Cleveland, Ohio—it felt like a torch had been passed down to me. A whisper from my Ancestors saying, "Yaaas, girl, yaaas! You have been called to be a voice for women of color. Empower yourself. Empower your sisters. Help them reach their wildest dreams."

And so, the seeds were planted and watered. I embraced my calling—a calling that has led me to many different projects over the course of my life and career. In 1986, I founded the Miss Black USA Pageant, the nation's first scholarship pageant for African American women, awarding over $500,000 in scholarships. I went on to cofound Diabetes Awareness Day in The Gambia, West Africa. I was appointed as a Goodwill Ambassador to the countries of The Gambia and Sierra Leone. I've mentored over a thousand young women, helping women to secure college scholarships, grants, and life-changing media and job opportunities.

While my work has taken many forms over the years, my goal is always the same: to help black women claim their power, redefine their destinies, and defy expectations.

We are living in a pivotal moment. For the first time in history, we've had an African American First Lady, a black woman on the top of Forbes Richest Women in Entertainment list, and sisters in positions of prestige and power at organizations like XEROX, Care USA, Microsoft, The Robert Wood Johnson Foundation and The World Bank.

So many victories. So much to celebrate. And yet, there's still so much work to be done. It's time to redefine what it means to be a courageous, compassionate, and confident black woman today. We've got obstacles to overcome, stereotypes to smash, and trauma to release. No question about it. The road forward won't be easy, but it will be worth it. So, my question for YOU is:

How BIG do you want to live?

It's time to dream bigger, think bigger, and live bigger. It's time to rise into what I call Your Next Level Life.

What is a "Next Level Life"? It means different things for different women. For you, hitting that next level might mean doubling or tripling your salary. It might mean buying a house for yourself—or a house for your parents. It might mean seeing your face on the cover of a magazine. It might mean contributing one thousand—or one million—dollars to a cause that you love. It might mean booking a trip to Dubai, securing a grant so you can take a three-month sabbatical and write your first book, or completing your BA, MA, or PhD. It might be a feeling in your gut, a feeling of worthiness and power.

With this book, I want to help you clarify what your Next Level Life looks and feels like and how to create it.

As you turn the page, I hope you will feel a spark igniting inside of you. The same spark that compelled me to protest at my high school, start the Miss Black USA Pageant, and write this book. The spark that burns with optimism and possibility and says, "It's time to live bigger and light the way for other women, too."

Your Next Level Life begins now.

RULE #1

IDENTIFY YOUR SUPERPOWERS

You were born with priceless gifts. You might have a natural knack for singing, teaching, making people laugh, or inspiring a community to take action. Find your superpowers, own them, and leverage them like crazy.

I believe every woman has a set of superpowers, waiting to be discovered.

Oprah Winfrey. Ava Duvernay. Michelle Obama. Kamala Harris. We all know these sisters and their superpowers.

What comes to mind when you think about Oprah? What are her greatest superpowers? Perhaps you think about her grounded presence, her confidence when she's speaking on camera, or her ability to build "something" where "nothing" stood before—to build a school, to build a media empire, to build a movement. And then there's Ava's creativity and imagination, Michelle's poise and grace under pressure, and Kamala's courage, tenacity, and grit.

Just like these incredible women, you were also born with priceless gifts. These innate talents are your superpowers. Oftentimes, these superpowers are hidden for a variety of reasons—perhaps because as a kid lots of adults told you to "tone it down" and "shut your mouth" or to "stick to the plan"; or because teachers told you that you were "too quiet" or "too loud" or just "too much"; or because your schools encouraged you to conform to the norm rather than shine; or because you were oppressed or neglected in some way, large or small.

Let me ask you a question:

Who were you before the world told you who you should be?

Can you remember?

That person—that shining, confident, radiant version of yourself—is where your superpowers reside. And if you're thinking, *I don't know if I've ever felt "radiant" and "confident" in my whole life*, that's OK. Even if they've been lost, suppressed, or forgotten, your superpowers can always be reclaimed again.

During the 2018 democratic primary, Alexandria Ocasio-Cortez, a little known, twenty-nine-year-old bartender and waitress from the Bronx, New York, beat out ten-term Democratic congressman Joe Crowley, the Democratic caucus chair. At the start of the Ocasio-Cortez campaign video, she says, "Women like me aren't supposed to run for office." Many said she was too young. She had not previously held elected office. She did not have access to wealth, social influence, or power. And she was hardly given any media time by the mainstream media.

But she didn't let that stop her. Age ain't nothing but a number to her. She went from no name to household name. From bartender to lawmaker. She tapped into her superpowers. And Netflix reportedly paid ten million dollars for a campaign documentary featuring the newly elected Congresswoman and Democratic party crasher. She connected with her community in an authentic way and used her tenacity, high energy, and emotional intelligence to become the youngest women to ever be elected to the US House of Representatives.

What are Ocasio-Cortez's superpowers? Her just-like-us relatability factor, oratorical skills, brilliance, fearlessness, and high-octane energy.

Alexandria Ocasio-Cortez is building her Next Level Life. It's all happening because she's using her superpowers instead of ignoring them.

If you're ready to live your Next Level Life, the first step is to identify your biggest superpowers, own them, and leverage them like crazy. Even when others have counted you out.

Not sure what your superpowers are? One of the best ways to discover your superpowers is to write down what fills you with joy. Not what fills your parents, friends, spouse, partner, mentor, or teachers with joy, but *you*.

Grab some paper and a pen and answer the following questions.

1. When do you feel the most alive?

2. When do you feel happy, energized, or full of joy?

3. What are your natural strengths—things you've always been good at?

4. What piques your curiosity? Are there topics, ideas, hobbies, pursuits, or activities that you feel naturally drawn to?

5. What types of praise or compliments do you tend to receive? (For example, do people compliment you for your patience, for your compassion, for your sense of humor, for your listening skills, for your impeccable organizational skills, for your creativity, or...perhaps something else?)

6. It's not always about breaking the rules but rewriting them instead. When you think about

the world as it currently is, what changes do you want to make?

As you roll through these questions, see if you notice any patterns, themes, or similarities.

Perhaps, like Ocasio-Cortez, you'll notice that political advocacy is when you shine brightest. Or perhaps, like me, you'll notice that mentoring and empowering other women is what brings you the greatest joy. Or perhaps you'll notice that there's a particular skill— writing, speaking, teaching, interviewing, coaching, inspiring, entertaining, leading, healing, supporting, nurturing, designing, building, fundraising, moving people to tears or laughter, making things aesthetically beautiful, or something else—that feels like a strong superpower for you.

Once you have identified your superpowers, it's time to leverage them.

Ask yourself, "How could I start using my superpowers every day? How could I start using my superpowers at my current job? In my community? How could I bring my superpowers into the center of my life and really use them, not ignore them?"

Leveraging your superpowers might feel scary, because it might mean stepping away from the plan that society has laid out for you. Feel the fear, but don't let it stop you. Claim your superpowers and start using them. This is the first big, brave step you must take—the first move toward your Next Level Life.

RULE #2

FIND YOUR NEXT
LEVEL FRIENDS

*Surround yourself with friends
who energize you, motivate you,
inspire you, open doors for you,
and make your world bigger.*

B ehind every female powerhouse is a tight-knit community of women lifting her higher. Oprah has Gayle. Bey has Solange. Speaking personally, I could not have achieved any of my biggest triumphs—including founding the Miss Black USA Pageant and Scholarship Foundation, or cofounding Diabetes Awareness Day in West Africa—without a strong tribe of sisters behind me.

I hope you've already got at least five amazing Gayle-level friends in your life. But, if you don't, now is the time to find those Next Level Friends—the spirit-awakening, butt-kicking, lift-you-up-higher-than-you've-ever-been-before women who will cheer you on and take you to new heights.

Call it a clan. Call it a tribe. Call it a family. No matter what you call it, it's going to bring you to a whole new level of success.

It's so powerful to have a circle of sisters waiting with open arms to elevate you, to help you articulate your dreams, to weigh in on ways you can get there, to grow your professional network, and to encourage you to step into a life full of impact and adventure. Sisters hold sacred space for you—and hold you accountable for your expansion into it. Sisters keep you going when you're ready to give in. Sisters see your blind spots, your best qualities, and your potential. Sisters see *you* as you are and as you are meant to be. And if you need a lil' devotion, they'll pray for you too.

Imagine what you could accomplish with the power of five badass ladies in your corner. You could:

- Write that book

- Leave that career in favor of one that fulfills you

- Heal that painful relationship

- Ask for that raise

- Give your first TED Talk

- Start that charity or six-figure start-up

- Visit that country

- Discover your superpowers and leverage them like crazy

Have you ever heard that you are the sum total of the five people you spend the most time with?

It's time to stop hanging with people who have your *problem* and time to start hanging with people who have your *solution*.

I remember who I was before I found my Next Level Gayle-friends and how far I've come since then. When I began to consciously build my sisterhood, it was as if the clouds parted in my favor. Having an attorney in my circle was not on my to-do list. But the day I met Lisa Walker, Esq., my game changed and net worth tripled. My brother suggested we meet, so I arranged a power lunch at a small Italian restaurant in my neighborhood with nothing on the agenda other than girl talk, good wine tasting, and risotto. Lisa, a very accomplished attorney, walked in the restaurant oozing with confidence (my mind went straight to Meghan Markle's character in *Suits*). I quickly pulled out pearls. Over the next three and half hours, we shared life stories, laughed, and charted a new course for my non-profit (and my Next Level Life). Some people are just gifted with genius, intuition, discernment, and the ability to cut through to the root of your stuff to pull out the "you" that you are meant to be. And that's Lisa on a whole other level. This sister is also licensed to practice law before the United

States Supreme Court. Just being in her presence makes you better.

As we departed the restaurant, Lisa paused, looked toward me, and said, "I'm going to be your attorney."

Waving hands to the sky, saying thank you to the Most High!

Since then, Lisa has become more than a legal advisor. She's a sister, confidante, mentor, and friend.

Note to self: Highly successful women think differently and can see your blind spots. There's not a single thing that happens in my life now that I don't consult with Lisa on or seek out her advice about. I've learned so much from her about being a boss, business negotiations, and life. She's even introduced me to her power network. Clearly the Universe knew who I needed in this new season of unlimited possibilities.

New opportunities arose from seemingly nowhere. I was introduced to people I'd always wanted to meet and invited to exotic destinations I'd always wanted to go. That's what I want for you, too.

Imagine what you could accomplish if you strategically cultivated your inner circle.

If you want to up-level your life and career, you've got to upgrade the quality of people you allow into your world. Surround yourself with grade-A encouragement, and you'll rise to the top. Surround yourself with complainers, pessimists, naysayer, bullies, losers, users, and abusers, and you'll sink to the lowest common denominator.

Who has your back? Who's your Gayle? Who are your Next Level Gayle-friends?

Today:

1. Identify the people who lift you up.

Write down the names of everyone in your inner circle of love and trust. Friends. Family. Teachers. Your pastor or spiritual mentor. Take a moment to thank each person for their continued love and encouragement. Send a text. Send a gift. Never take these people for granted.

2. Identify the people who drag you down.

Take a good, hard look at the relationships in your life that pull you down. Relationships that exhaust you, drain you, or leave you feeling weakened instead of strong. These people are NOT your Next Level Friends. Sooner or later, you'll need to eliminate—or renegotiate—those relationships. Your confidence and success depend on it.

3. Reach out to one person you'd like to know better.

You know that fabulous, shining, charismatic, confident woman that you've admired from afar? The woman who's using her superpowers to the fullest? Reach out. Invite her to an event. Congratulate her on one of her recent victories. Or tell her about your latest project. Invite her into your life and see if she's open to sparking (or deepening) a friendship with you.

When you upgrade your circle of friends, you upgrade your entire life.

RULE #3

EXPAND YOUR HORIZONS

How to expand your mind (and unlock new doors) with travel, networking, mentoring, and hidden opportunities you might not even know about.

Mindset is everything.

Most of us spend so much time focusing on the problem instead of the solution.

We obsess over the door that's locked ("Nooo! Why???") instead of looking at the wide-open window that's right there, just two feet away.

This is the type of mindset that's keeping you from stepping into your Next Level Life. Instead of saying, "How am I going to do this?" we need to start saying, "I know there's a way to do this. Maybe I don't see it yet, but I'll figure it out. I can't wait to see how this unfolds." We need an expansive mindset, not a constricted one.

It's the things that we can't see that lead us to our ultimate destination. Ruth didn't look back to what was familiar, she stepped out on faith. Courage brought her to her divine destiny. So often, in our lives, obstacles are merely opportunities in disguise.

Losing my so-called dream job was one of the best things that ever happened to me. Of course, it didn't seem like it at the time. Over and over again, I kept asking myself, *Why did this happen to me? What am I going to do now? How am I going to pay my bills?*

I had just purchased a new car, and the monthly payments weren't cheap. How was I going to pay for it with no income? But the flipside was that losing my job forced me to think differently. It forced me to think outside the box. It forced me to step outside my comfort zone. It also taught me that when times get tough, your network is worth more than gold. Or, as I like to say, your network is your net worth.

Even in the midst of my unemployed panic-state, I understood that worrying never solves anything; action does. So I set up a lunch date with a colleague who worked for the same company. Yes, the same company I used to work at, prior to being let go. I respected my colleague's opinions and valued her friendship. Not once did she ever allow me to shrink, think small, or give up. In fact, oftentimes, she had more confidence in my abilities than I did.

During our lunch, she suggested that I present a proposal to the powers that be, outlining a role for myself as a consultant. We decided to rewrite my previous job description and take it to a whole new level. A six-figure salary (a 50 percent salary increase). First class travel benefits (hello, frequent flier miles). Luxury accommodation in a five-star hotel (every Monday through Friday). A generous expense account (all meals on them). Crazy, right?

As we wrote up the proposal, I definitely had a few moments where I thought to myself, *This is insane.* This company had just ended my position. Now here I was, with the nerve to reach out and pitch myself as a pricey consultant? Would they laugh in my face? Was this a ridiculous plan? My heart pounded in my chest. It took a week before I found the courage to hit send.

Within six hours of sending the proposal, I received a response from the person at the top. My proposal was approved. Turns out, they needed the services I could provide. They had the budget to make it happen. The CEO thought it was a win-win situation and approved every stipulation, including the six-figure salary. I was overjoyed and pretty stunned. *WTH just happened?*

This was a defining moment in my life, because this was the moment when I learned that it's possible to turn a devastating loss into a divine blessing and a lesson. I also learned the power of just asking. So often, in life, we're terrified to just send the darn email and ask. You have not because you ask not. If you think small, you get small. If you think BIG, you get BIG. I went from "fired" to favor and "first class airfare" with the opportunity to design my own life, on my terms, all because I found the courage to ask for it.

When you change the way you look at things, the things you look at change.

Today, you have a blank slate. You must master a new way to think and train your mind to see the good in everything.

Create the highest, grandest vision for your life, and let every step you take move you in that direction. When obstacles are thrown your way, use them as building blocks to create opportunities you never imagined.

The key word here is create. Create is a verb: an action word. It's all about doing.

Most people think that with enough brains, talent, and charisma, success will eventually arrive. Not quite. We have to take action.

You can be the most beautiful natural-hair woman in the world—but if you don't enter that modeling competition, how are you going to win?

You can be the most brilliant woman in the room—but if you don't apply for that college scholarship or grant, how are you going to get it?

You can be funnier than Tiffany Haddish and Nicole Byer combined—but if you don't sign up for that acting class or register for an open-mic night at a comedy club, how is a talent agent ever going to discover you?

If you've been waiting for a waving sign, this is it.

Today:

- Take one step toward creating an opportunity you want.

- Expand your network. Expand your world. Expand your sense of what's possible.

- If you're aiming for a new job, set up a meeting with a career counselor.

- If you're trying to launch a business, make an appointment at your local SCORE chapter to get paired up with a business mentor for free.

- If you're craving more fulfillment and meaning, find a local charity and fill out a volunteer application. Better still, give yourself permission to create your own charity.

- If you're unemployed—or if you feel lost and don't know what to do with your life—set up a lunch date with someone whose opinion you respect. Ask questions and listen. Your friend might suggest a path you hadn't even considered. A lunch date can change your whole life. (It certainly changed mine.)

- If you're seeking a mentor, one of the best ways to attract stronger role models, teachers, and mentors into your world is to become a mentor yourself.

- You want to travel internationally but don't have the budget right now? Apply *stat* for a Visa or ATM debit reward card and rack up those miles to earn a free flight—or apply for a side gig with an airline for the free flight benefits.

Make no secret of your ambitions. Own it. Testify. Tell three people in your power entourage precisely what you want to create. Invite them to support you as you step into a life of greater impact, faith, and service. (Be prepared for yasss, girl, yasss!)

There are billions of people in this world and billions of opportunities too. Don't sequester yourself in your house with the doors shut and the lights turned off. Keep reaching out and speaking up. Keep connecting. Keep signing up for new classes and experiences.

Keep making your world bigger, and you'll discover hidden opportunities that you'd never even considered before.

RULE #4

MAGNETIZE MONEY

*How to create all the money you
need through grants, sponsors,
scholarships, and entrepreneurial gold.*

W ealth is your birthright.
Despite the passage of the Equal Pay Act of 1968 and the Lilly Ledbetter Fair Pay Act of 2009, women are still not receiving equal pay for equal work. Women are still fighting for their fair share of wealth and still staggering behind men. And for women of color the gap is even wider.

While these truths are sobering, the silver lining is that there has never been a greater time in history for women to become fabulously wealthy. Do we live in a perfect society? No. Is everything fair? No. However, today, more than ever before, women have more opportunities to create wealth.

Money is out there. It's everywhere. It's available for you to claim. Billions of dollars in scholarships, grants, and entrepreneurial gold are awarded annually and can be found online. Make the internet your bae.

Nothing is out of your reach. You can buy your dream home, pursue an advanced degree, launch your own dream business, and travel the world—seated in business class, honey. I'm here to tell you, you can have it all.

Part of building wealth is building your skillset. Need to up-level your communication, problem-solving, or writing skills or learn a new language? There are hundreds of free courses online. Harvard, Princeton, University of Pennsylvania, and other Ivy League schools offer a variety of courses on the web through edX (www.edx.org) and Coursera (www.coursera.org). Take a class. Become an expert. Boss up your resume. These courses are free and self-paced so you can start learning today.

One of the most exciting things about studying a new subject is how it expands your mind and unlocks new career (and new money-making) opportunities. You just never know where one course might lead.

While taking a graduate course on women's health in small communities, I discovered that heart disease is the leading cause of death for women in my own town. I was moved to fight back. I created a plan—an online initiative to improve access to quality preventive healthcare for women in my community. I had data, I had solutions, and I had passion, but I wasn't sure where to secure funding to launch the initiative. I placed "get funding" further down on my to-do list.

A year later, while scrolling online, I came across an organization called Ladies Who Launch—a networking site for fearless entrepreneurial women, providing them with the tools, resources, and connections to start a business or grow existing ventures. There was a webpage dedicated to grants and other funding opportunities. On that page, I noticed a grant opportunity for women sponsored by Jones New York, the fashion company.

This grant was the perfect match for my women's health initiative. I looked over the application and noticed the deadline was that same day. I had less than two hours to meet the deadline. I could have decided, *Oh well, it's too late*, but something in my gut urged me to pull myself together and make this happen. I quickly researched the previous year's winners. Most of them were high-profile executives at Fortune 500 companies, big hotshots, non-profit game changers. The odds of me winning were looking pretty slim. I'm thinking, *How can I compete with these incredible women?*

Well, I'll tell you how. First, I formed a one-woman prayer circle. Then, I started cracking away at my application, working as quickly as I could—because the clock was counting down! I'm a believer in taking risks.

I knew my initiative had the potential to touch—and even save—thousands of lives. My initiative was that d*mn good. The initiative wasn't about me. It was about a cause greater than myself. And maybe that is the answer to attracting and manifesting what we want in our life. Make it less about "me" and more about serving. I wanted to empower women to improve the quality of their health. That was my objective.

So, I refused to shrink. I poured my whole heart and soul into the application, explaining that heart disease was more than a statistic—it was claiming the lives of real women. Mothers, daughters, sisters with names. I even listed a few names—actual people who'd been lost too soon. Women who could have been saved.

I figured, *I've done my best. All the judges could do is say "no." And I've heard "no" before. It won't kill me.* I finished the application literally three minutes before the five o'clock deadline and hit the send button.

Two weeks later, I received an email from Jones New York with "Winners" listed in the subject line. I opened the email. Shocked and in disbelief, I saw my name listed next to six others. I was awarded one of seven Jones

New York women's empowerment grants. Several weeks later, the grant check arrived in the mail and I began the work I was called to do—a full-on fight to combat heart disease and improve women's health in my community. The following week, I got another astounding package in the mail. It was a boss wardrobe from Jones New York that Kerry Washington would have approved. Power suits and creamy cashmere sweaters and crisp CEO-level shirts and blazers, oh-my-gaaawd!

In the coming weeks, all of the honorees participated in a professional photoshoot and were featured on the Jones New York website. *Vanity Fair* sponsored an exclusive lunch in our honor at a luxury hotel in Washington, DC. I networked with a room full of awe-inspiring women and formed a new sisterhood. The lunch ended with an introduction to Dee Dee Myers, my new business mentor and the first female press secretary in the White House under President Bill Clinton. This one grant opportunity led to numerous other opportunities. I went from overlooked to overbooked.

Every year, hundreds of grants, scholarships, and opportunities are announced online from corporations, organizations, and government agencies.

I've learned that money is not scarce. Money is everywhere. You just have to raise your hand and claim it. Claim it—and then use it to improve your life, improve your community, and do great things in the world.

Make this your new money anthem:

"I am a magnet for divine abundance in the form of money, health, and happiness."

Ready to go back to school, earn an advanced degree, or travel abroad? Listen up. There are scholarships for everyone. Working moms, single moms, divorced moms, women under thirty, women over sixty: you name it, there's a scholarship for you. You can find all of them online. My niece was awarded over $1.5 million in scholarships this last year. For real.

Always remember that having a job is one way to earn money. Getting a grant or scholarship is another. But don't limit yourself to a bi-weekly paycheck or a one-time check in the mail. There are unlimited ways to make money. Think outside the box. Think non-traditional. Consider launching a business. Or put together a website and position yourself as a corporate consultant. Consider public speaking. You can deliver an inspiring keynote and get paid five figures to speak on stage for one hour. Consider writing a book. Producing an event. Inventing a product. Opening a side-business that you run two days a week. So many options. Why limit yourself?

Earning more money is all about expanding your horizons (we talked about this in the previous section, as you might remember), taking new risks, and putting yourself in new situations. For instance, I've noticed that whenever I travel internationally, money comes pouring my way. Once I'm thirty-five thousand feet up in the air, something magical happens to my bank account. On my last trip to the Middle East, I sat next to a human rights attorney on the plane. After learning about the work that I do, he sent numerous speaking and international travel opportunities my way. Cha-ching! That flight paid for itself, many times over!

Bottom line: to be able to afford anything, you don't always need a day job or a side hustle. Think even more expansively. Take advantage of the resources you'll find online. It's incredible what you can do with a computer, Wi-Fi, and a few hours of your time. You can launch a website. Set up an online shop. Apply for a life-changing grant. Email a potential investor. It's all out there and somebody's going to get that money—why shouldn't it be you?

Whatever your goal, there's a grant, scholarship, or opportunity to match. With the right attitude, you can magnetize all the money you need. A life-altering five- or six-figure grant—or some other equally exciting opportunity—might be just one application and two hours away. Get out there and claim it!

RULE #5

POSITION YOURSELF
LIKE A STAR

*The secrets of self-presentation.
How to style yourself, promote
yourself with elegance, and
feel amazingly confident.*

As the founder of the Miss Black USA Pageant, I've coached some of the most elegant, glamorous, and well-spoken women in the nation—women who are far more than just "beauty queens," but community leaders, scholars, and rising artists. They're amplifying their voices, and the world is taking note. Because when you show up—confident—in six-inch heels and red lipstick, you give other women permission to show up in a *big* way, too.

Do you want to command attention, land that promotion, dazzle an audience, or score that big gig? Talent, intelligence, and personal conviction count—but you've got to package yourself powerfully too, from your clothes, to your message, to your posture. That's how you'll seal the deal.

Approach everything you do as if you're auditioning for the starring role. Channel your inner Ciara, Bey, Kerry, Taraji, Michelle, and O! It might sound silly, but practice walking across your bedroom with Queen Bey-level confidence and grace. Walk, walk, walk, and pose. Be you. Be authentic. Be unapologetic. When you walk into a room, let every inch of your body say, "I'm heeeeerrre!" Take five steps across the room and pretend you're walking onto a TV set for your big interview. Pretend you're walking into the White House. Pretend you're walking onstage to give a speech at the Essence Festival. How would you walk? How would you wave? How would you smile and carry yourself in that moment? Practice until it doesn't feel silly, until it just feels real and right.

Confidence is everything. When a woman walks into the room, her confidence must arrive first. Consider a woman like Meghan Markle. The *Suits* star went from TV actor to the Duchess of Sussex. And she did it flawlessly, being true to her roots.

Just when you thought Michelle Obama's star power couldn't rise any higher, she released her best-seller *Becoming*. The former First Lady and Barack's better half got all the rave reviews on the final stop of her book tour where she stunned in four-thousand-dollar killer gold Balenciaga thigh-high boots and a bright yellow silk shirt maxi dress. Though Michelle is no longer First Lady her star power is undeniable! When she opens her mouth, the world listens. She presents herself like a warrior, like a champion, like the shining star that she is.

A Few Time-Tested Secrets

Dress like you already have the job. (And when I say "job," I mean the job, grant, scholarship, prize, client, agent, book deal, TV deal, whatever you want most.)

Act like you already have the job.

Speak like you already have the job.

May all your vibes say, "I got this." Energy is contagious.

Find your voice. Use it and amplify it like Forever First Lady Michelle Obama.

Find a cause you're passionate about. Appoint yourself as the official spokesperson.

When you're genuinely passionate about something, then you never have to "fake it." You feel naturally confident. It radiates from within. Your tone of voice always feels strong and powerful.

Embrace your unique style.

Nurture your body, mind, and spirit.

If you're a curvy girl, there is no reason to hide and every reason to flaunt your feel-good, body-positive vibes.

If you've never gotten professional headshots taken, get on that! Get some beautiful shots that you're proud to show off.

And please, get undergarments that fit correctly. I can't emphasize this enough. The right bra will transform your shape, make you stand taller, and help you feel put together from the inside out. Cherry Blossom Intimates, cofounded by beauty pageant veteran Jasmine Jones and breast-care surgeon Dr. Regina Hampton, is one company I especially love. They carry sizes from 28AA to 52N and their social media campaigns feature a refreshingly diverse group of women of all shades and body types. It's amazing how a little bit of lace and some underwire can shift your whole day!

Above all, love yourself. Look in the mirror and say something kind to yourself. Take good care of yourself. Treat yourself like a queen. Whether you are natural, curly, or straight-haired, light skinned or dark skinned, or any of the fifty thousand beautiful shades of brown, love the skin you're in.

Tips from a Makeup Artist to the Stars

When I think of women with star power, of course, I think about women like Michelle Obama and Oprah. When these women walk in a room, the energy shifts. It's as if the stars have aligned. And it goes without saying, these women always look amazing! Hair and make-up are always on point. They're always glowing like they came fresh from a Canyon Ranch spa.

What's their secret? I consulted with my good friend Derrick Rutledge, a master make-up artist who has an A-list client roster, including two of the nation's most photographed faces—Michelle Obama and Oprah—as well as singers such as Patti LaBelle, Shirley Caesar and CeCe Winans. For eighteen months, Rutledge spent every day in the East Wing with Michelle Obama. Shortly thereafter, he got the call and now has the number one spot on Oprah's beauty speed-dial. Rutledge has a way of bringing out the best in his clients. Beauty. Confidence. The glow of stardom.

Rutledge offers the following insider tips on helping you to feel confident:

- To get that star power glow, take iridescent, nude-colored blush or bronzer and hit the apples of your cheeks, forehead, chin, and center of your nose with a brush. It will give you a fresh all-over glow.

- Dress to impress, he says. But make sure you're comfortable. If those stiletto heels are pinching your feet and making you want to cry, that's not going to boost your confidence. Wear something that feels good on your skin. Confidence is all about how you feel and how you carry yourself.

I couldn't agree more with Rutledge's advice. Bottom line: you are a queen. Dress, speak, act, and present yourself accordingly. Even if you're currently making minimum wage or struggling to land your first client or desperately trying to find a scholarship, present yourself like a star. Take pride in your appearance. Take those extra five minutes in the morning to make sure your eyeliner is popping. Put on those fabulous earrings that your grandma gave to you. Little touches can make a big difference in how you feel and how you interact with others. Even if you're working in an entry-level position right now, when you walk into the office, you want everyone to assume, *Oh, she must be the boss.*

When you carry yourself like a boss, pretty soon, you become the boss. As the ancient Greek philosopher Heraclitus says, "Day by day, what you do is who you become." Do whatever you need to do to feel like a star. And that's exactly who you will become.

RULE #6

KEEP IT REAL

How to close the gap between what you're saying and what you're actually doing.

I founded the Miss Black USA Pageant back in 1986. Since that year, I've had conversations with over a thousand young women—conversations about their aspirations, their education, their future goals, everything they want to be and achieve. I'm constantly encouraging women to think bigger. I'm the queen of preaching, "Dream big!"

Of course, it's easy to talk about big dreams. But, it's harder to walk the talk and put your dreams into action and move toward your goals. Now, don't get me wrong. Talking big and dreaming a big life are the beginnings to every earth-shaking action that ever took place throughout history and always will be. Talking things out is the first step toward building Your Next Level Life.

Unfortunately, most people are unable to move beyond the big talk and launch into action. That's because they probably think of their dreams and goals as these huge undertakings and put unnecessary pressure on themselves to get from A to Oprah instantly.

But Oprah wasn't built in a day!

Don't expect to reach your goal overnight. The key to closing the gap between your dreams and your reality is to break down what you're saying you want to do "eventually" into easily attainable chunks of action that you can do right now.

Here are my top seven recommendations on how to close the gap between what you're saying and what you're actually doing:

1. Create a ninety-day road map.

Ask yourself, "What can I do in the next ninety days to get closer to my dream? How can I get from point A to point B, or maybe C or D?" If ninety days feels too overwhelming, make it five or ten days, whatever timeframe feels doable for you.

2. Focus on what you can do today.

Focus on small, immediate steps that you can take right now, today, with whatever resources you currently have. Can you apply online for a scholarship right now? You sure can! Can you spend thirty minutes researching job opportunities right now? Yes, ma'am! Can you schedule a coffee date with a career counselor right now? Yaaaas! Can you take a quick walk around the block or find a cardio workout video on YouTube and follow along in your living room right now? Yup.

You don't need money or special privileges or connections to do any of these things. You can just do it. Get moving today. That's the key. Keep asking yourself, "What can I do today?"

3. Start scheduling action steps on your calendar.

It's one thing to say, "Oh yeah, I'm going to the gym…" and another to make a date with a fitness friend, lock it into your calendar, and make it a real appointment. If you're serious about your dreams, make things official. Put the steps you need to take right onto your calendar. If "Get car oil changed" and "Get hair done" go onto your calendar, then your biggest dreams deserve a place on your calendar too.

For example, one of my goals right now is to have more quality time with the people I love. Here's what I'm putting on my calendar: A FaceTime session with my son who lives three thousand miles away. See a stand-up comedy show with a dear friend. More QT with my mom, including a destination spa weekend. Once those experiences are on my calendar, I know they are going to happen.

4. Celebrate the small victories.

Once you've hit your first milestone, you'll be so proud of yourself. Acknowledge and celebrate your small victory—whatever it is!

Maybe you got your first rejection letter from a magazine. They didn't want to publish your article, but they gave positive feedback and encouraged you to keep writing. OK, it's not the response you wanted, but it's a small victory nonetheless because at least you're walking down your path, taking action, and getting closer to where you want to be!

Or maybe you've experienced an even happier victory— your first email saying, "We'd love to have you stop by for a job interview" or "Let's meet for lunch to discuss your proposal" or "You're a Semi-Finalist." Hallelujah! Take a moment to celebrate this win. Let it sink in.

This momentum will carry you to the next milestone and the next and the next until you reach your goal. It will feel like "winning" all along. And that's the real goal to all of this, isn't it? To enjoy the journey and to fill every moment with passion and inspiration and love.

5. Make it fun!

Stop making your journey a chore and start making it fun and inspiring. If you're going to spend five hours of your life researching scholarships or colleges online for example, you don't have to do it in a dreary bedroom with the curtains drawn shut and the lights turned off. Make it fun! Make it beautiful! Open the windows. Breathe in the fresh air. Light a candle. Play some Rihanna. Invite a friend over to work on her laptop right alongside you and make it a double-research date. There's always a way to make "doing the work" a little more fun.

Too often, we allow our big dreams to block our path, and we never see them through. Don't fall into that trap. Make your dreams a reality by laying one stone at a time (girl, make sure that stone is a diamond) and loving each stone with all you've got. You'll be amazed at what you can create when you let go of fear and doubt and let passion and joy take over.

6. Make forgiveness a daily ritual.

Perhaps a teacher, family member, friend, or significant other once told you you weren't good enough. But you are. It's so easy to believe that naysaying inner voice that insists you can't, you won't, you suck, it'll never happen. Break the stronghold. Forgive them.

Forgive whoever hurt you, whoever lied to you, or whoever tried to dim your brilliant shine. Let it go. Forgiveness doesn't mean what this person did was "OK" or "acceptable" or that they're allowed to do it again. Forgiveness doesn't necessarily mean that this person is invited to continue being part of your life. Forgiveness simply means that you're deciding to release the heavy burden of pain and sadness and say, "I'm choosing to let this go. I'm choosing to forgive and move on, because I want to feel lighter and happier and free." Forgiveness is a gift that you give to yourself.

And yes, sometimes the hardest person to forgive is yourself. But it's so important. If you're carrying around a thousand pounds of anger and disappointment about yourself—anger about all the mistakes you've made, the opportunities you've squandered, the steps you should have taken five years ago—guess what? That thousand-pound weight on your back is just going to slow you down and make it harder to reach your new destination. Let it go. Release the weight. Say, "I'm not perfect. I've made some poor decisions, but that's in the past. My past doesn't define who I am today, or where I'm going. Every day, I'm choosing to work a little harder and be my best self!" With that kind of attitude, you'll be able to move toward your new dreams so much faster.

You are awesome. You are worthy. You are deserving. The world can no longer hold you back from what is yours.

7. Stay open-minded.

It's great to make plans. But sometimes God, the Universe, whatever term you prefer, has a different set of plans for you. And sometimes, as you're walking down your path, new opportunities arise that you'd never even considered.

Back when I was an eighteen-year-old college student, I never "planned" to get involved with the fight against heart disease and diabetes. I never "planned" to start a pageant. I never "planned" to organize a conference for two hundred badass women in Dubai. I never "planned" to do 90 percent of the things I've done! All of those opportunities and projects arose later, sometimes very unexpectedly.

So, it's great to set ambitious goals—but don't be upset if you end up deviating from your intended destination. Sometimes diversions lead to more exciting places and experiences that you could never imagine on your own. Sometimes plans change. Be flexible. Be open to new experiences. Write your plans in pencil.

Write down one of your top goals:

_____

_____

_____

Break this goal down into five to seven steps that you can complete over the next ninety days. Focus on small steps that you can do right now, immediately, with the resources that you currently have.

1. _____

2. _____

3. _____

4. _____

5. _____

6. _____

7. _____

Get moving. Less talking, more doing.

RULE #7

GIVE BACK
FROM DAY ONE

*Don't wait until "someday later"
to serve the world. Begin on day one.
Become a mentor and share
what you've learned. Become
a philanthropist or champion a
cause. Help other women to rise.*

've always believed in the concept of lifting as you climb. Helping others is not only a good thing to do, it makes you feel happy and healthier too. The most fulfilling, life-changing, and transformative experiences I've ever had came from serving others.

I never set out to be a philanthropist specifically. I just set out to do good and make a difference. But philanthropy has given me a chance to check so many things off my bucket list. Like traveling around the world. Meeting one-on-one with foreign heads of states. Getting featured in a glossy magazine. Meeting my favorite heroes and celebrities. All of these "OMG!" moments came into my life, because I was on the path of philanthropy and service. Doing good brings so much good back to you.

Get into the spirit of giving and your life will blossom and unfold in ways that you could never imagine. Here's one example of how this happened for me...

It was on my first visit to the African continent that I found my calling. The moment I stepped off the plane and onto African soil, I could hear the Ancestors saying, "Welcome home." The number one must-have experience on my travel itinerary—after brunching on chicken yassa—was to pay a visit to a local hospital. I've always felt a deep, spiritual responsibility to help people, so I arranged a tour with the medical director of a public community hospital.

As I toured the crumbling facilities and watched patients laying helpless, I was moved to serve. I felt a calling that I couldn't ignore. I returned home and shared my experience with my personal physician, Dr. Dawne Carroll, and she was inspired to help, too.

Since diabetes is the number one cause of death in The Gambia, we decided to team up and sponsor The Gambia's first-ever Diabetes Awareness Day. The goal was to educate, test, and treat as much of the local population as possible. We partnered with The Royal Victoria Teaching Hospital, located in a poverty-stricken area of the country's capital of Banjul. Due to the hospital's inadequate financial resources, logistical support, and trained staff, we were presented with an insurmountable task.

Determined to make it happen, I took on fundraising, refusing to accept no for an answer. Dr. Carroll pulled out all stops and tapped into her own network of pharmaceutical reps who service her two private family medicine practices. They came through with large donations of testing supplies, drugs, and medical equipment. I successfully raised the money needed to cover our flights, materials, shipping, and other administrative costs. Dr. Carroll generously donated her time and arrived with her trained staff in tow. We created a day-long public health event to raise awareness about the disease and to provide testing and treatment for the local population. At the end of the day, over three hundred citizens were educated, tested, and treated. Lives were saved on this day—and my life was forever changed.

Nobody invited me to cofound Diabetes Awareness Day. Nobody emailed me to pitch the idea. Nobody texted me to say, "Will you help?" This was an opportunity that I created for myself, and I'm so grateful I did.

When you take charge of your destiny and create opportunities for yourself, unbelievable rewards come to you. One opportunity unlocks another, then another, and another.

For example, after leading Diabetes Awareness Day, I was named a goodwill ambassador to The Gambia by

His Excellency, the president of The Gambia. This was an unimaginable honor that brought me to tears—and of course, this never would have happened unless I set out to do good.

You Already Have What It Takes

Many people believe that they don't have what it takes to make a difference to the world. They believe only people like Oprah, Mahatma Gandhi, Mother Teresa, Bill Gates, and the like are capable of making a difference.

The truth is, every one of us is put on this world to contribute and make a difference in our own unique way. It doesn't necessarily need to be something enormous. It just needs to be something you do with the intention of "doing good."

Don't have the extra cash to max out your karmic potential? Give your time.

Ever looked at a picture of a young girl or boy in Africa and, short of filling out adoption papers, you wanted to save the child? All you need is a computer and a webcam to mentor a young child. Infinite Family (infinitefamily. org) is a video mentoring site that connects volunteers with African preteens and teens. To join, simply fill out an application, complete the online training, and get access to a secure intranet for weekly video dates. Conversations occur between eight o'clock in the morning and noon US time. You can make a life-changing difference in a child's life simply by showing up to say, "Hi sweetheart. How are you?"

Visit VisoGive (youtube.com/user/give), YouTube's nonprofit channel. Charities upload fun videos and earn 60 percent of the ad revenue when you watch. It's much more meaningful than watching clips of cats riding skateboards!

Got just a couple of minutes? Make them count. Visit Sparked (skillsforchange.com), a volunteering site for professionals, while you're waiting in line at the grocery store or waiting for a barista to make your coffee. This website offers lots of volunteering options based on how much time you have available—five minutes, thirty minutes, two hours, whatever you can spare. You can offer ideas for a nonprofit's fundraiser, write a letter to an underprivileged child, create a new logo for an organization that can't afford a graphic designer, and more. You'll get a weekly email with options based on your interests. Or search the site by cause or location to choose an activity.

What are you passionate about?

What can you do today?

What gifts or talents do you have that you can share?

Don't wait until "someday later" to serve the world. Don't wait until you're richer than Oprah or Bill Gates. Don't wait until you have more connections or more time or more of whatever you think you need. Begin now. No matter your age or economic status, you have something that you can share. Become a mentor and teach what you've learned. Help other women to rise. Become a philanthropist or champion a cause.

When you commit to a lifetime of service, the world sends unimaginable rewards in your direction. Begin now. Give back from day one. Help other people to build their own Next Level Life…as you build yours.

ARE YOU
LEVELING UP?

Write to Me and Tell Me How

Thank you for reading *Your Next Level Life*.

I hope this short book inspired you to make some big leaps in your life. And I would love to hear from you. For real.

Head over here…

karenarrington.com/contact

…and send me an email anytime.

Tell me exactly how you're building your Next Level Life. What action steps are you taking? Did you make a list of your strongest superpowers? Have you applied for a scholarship or grant? Did you upgrade your personal style or beauty regime? Did you reach out to a woman you'd love to know, because maybe she could become your soulmate-friend, the Gayle to your Oprah?

Tell me about the steps you're taking. And, if you're not into email, follow me on Instagram (@karen_arrington) and talk to me there!

RESOURCES

Beauty, Branding, and Presentation

Dr. Myla Bennett: The founder of Ederra Bella Plastic Surgery & Medical Spa is a surgeon, skin care expert, and creator of the Preserve Your Pretty campaign, which empowers women to celebrate their inner pretty. Visit ederrabella.com.

Derrick Rutledge: Master makeup artist to Oprah Winfrey. His five-figure daily rates may be out of your budget, but follow him on Instagram and get all of the beauty inspo you need: @derrick4mkup.

Balancing Beautiful Bodies: Because being healthy and fit is a lifestyle. Balancingbeautifulbodies.com.

Cherry Blossom Intimates: Cofounded by Jasmine Jones and Dr. Regina Hampton, this is a chic lingerie boutique that you'll love. Say buh-bye to boring beige bras. Every woman deserves to feel beautiful, no matter her bra size or her breast cancer status. Cherryblossomintimates.com.

Nude Barre: Eco-friendly intimates made in twelve shades of nude to match every skin tone. Nudebarre.com.

Joelle Polisky: Pitching and national media placements are her jam! Connect with her at jpolisky12@gmail.com.

Alexandra Franzen: When you're ready to outline your TEDx talk, write your book, and play big, hire Alex. She often has a waiting list a year long, and she's worth the wait. Alexandrafranzen.com.

Vonecia Carswell: Because you need ridiculously gorgeous headshots stat. Get in touch with V Studios at voneciacarswell.com.

Beverli Alford: You don't have to stand five foot ten to shoot with this *America's Next Top Model* photographer. Photography is her superpower. Don't wait. Book her today. Beverlialfordphotography.com.

The SuperpowHer Podcast: Media personality Deya Direct gets real with celebrities and power players on how they leverage their superpowers. Real talk. Deyadirect.net/podcast.

The McGhee Law Firm: It's never been easier to get your business up and running. Protect your dream and your brand at The McGhee Law Firm. Ask for the boss attorney Kyona McGhee, Esq. Check out themcgheelawfirm.com or find Kyona on Instagram: @kyonathelawyer.

Natascha Saunders: Need a resume? Need help navigating financial aid or the college admissions process? As a certified career coach, she's your woman. Nataschasaunders.com/services.html.

Scholarships, Personal Finance, and Free Money

Girl Boss Foundation Grant: $15,000. Grants are awarded on a biannual basis to individuals pursuing entrepreneurial endeavors. Apply at girlboss.com/foundation.

Nakia Sanford: This former WNBA star knows a lot about zeros on the front of a check and how you too can accumulate wealth. Visit primerica.com/nakiasanford.

Cartier Women's Initiative Award: $30,000 to $100,000. The Cartier Women's Initiative Award is awarded to eighteen female entrepreneurs around the world in the early stages of development of their business. Apply at cartierwomensinitiative.com.

Daphne Lee Artistic Legacy Award: $2,500. The scholarship is open to any female of color who is a full-time artist or student pursuing a degree in the performing arts in the US. Learn more at missblackusa. org/scholarship.

CBC Spouses Education Scholarship: Scholarships go to academically talented and highly motivated students of all majors who intend to pursue full-time undergraduate, graduate, or doctoral degrees. Apply at cbcfinc.org/ scholarships.

Thurgood Marshall College Fund: Multiple scholarships available. Look around and apply at tmcf.org.

L'Oréal USA For Women in Science: This fellowship program awards five female postdoctoral scientists with an annual grant of $60,000 each for their contributions in science, technology, engineering and math (STEM) fields. Apply at www.lorealusa.com/csr-commitments/ l'oréal-usa-for-women-in-science-program.

Unclaimed Money: Find unclaimed funds held by the government that might be owed to you. Start your search for money that might be yours by going to unclaimed.org.

Farefetch: This company will pay you to find cheap airfare deals. Get that $$$. Farefetch.com.

Pat Long: Investing in real estate can be a very smart move. She is a broker and co-owner of the first African American owned Keller Williams branch in Prince George's County, Maryland, with over five hundred agents. Patricialong.yourkwagent.com.

Sheila Rugege-Dantzler: A real estate broker at Jameson Sotheby's International Realty, you may have seen her on *House Hunters* on HGTV or as a frequent real estate expert on Fox 32 Chicago. This former Miss Black USA competitor has closed approximately seventy million dollars' worth of real estate. She can be reached at (312) 832-2300 or (312) 399-9056.

Free Medical School Tuition at Kaiser Permanente School of Medicine - The School will waive all tuition and fees for the entering classes of 2020 through 2024. This waiver will be available for each class for their four years

of enrollment. https://medschool.kp.org/admissions/
tuition-and-financial-aid

Amal Clooney Award - The new award will shine a light
on the unsung heroes who are the driving force behind
initiatives that are helping their communities to thrive.
To apply, visit http://princestrustinternational.org/
news1/princes-trust-international-introduces-the-amal-
clooney-award-a-global-youth-can-do-it-campaign/

On Camera Audiences - You can be a part of the live
studio audience of your fave TV show and win BIG!
OK, being a TV show audience member is not exactly a
"career plan"...but it can definitely be really fun and who
knows? Oprah might have an incredible surprise stashed
under your seat! Get your free tickets at www.on-camera-
audiences.com

Pageantry

Miss Black USA: Because little brown girls need to see
positive images of young women who look like them.
Awarding over $500,000 in scholarships to date at
missblackusa.org.

Miss HBCU Alumni Hall of Fame Pageant: This competition highlights and celebrates the queens of the nation's predominate and historical black colleges and universities. Black girl magic at its finest. Nbcahof.org.

Travel

Next Level Power Trip: A life-changing luxury travel adventure with me and other women who will become your BFFs for life. Expand your horizons with a trip to Milan, Dubai, or…who knows where we're going next? Check my website for the latest details. karenarrington.com.

Keenya Hofmaier: She visited Paris and never returned home. Paris will do that to you. Follow the former beauty queen and the founder of Black Expats in Paris at keenyahofmaier.com.

Paris Talks: If you're Paris-obsessed (like Keenya) check out this conference on the future of humanity and why Paris is always a good idea. Apply to become a speaker at paris-talks.com/speakers/become-a-speaker.

Anesu Mbizvo, MD: She is changing the face of yoga. This former physician returned to her first love and launched The Nest Space Yoga Studio in Johannesburg, South Africa. If you're traveling there, definitely visit. Learn more at thenestspace.co.za.

JetSuiteX: You don't have to be a member of the 2 percent club to travel like them. Fly private with fares starting at $129. The small print: Flights are available only between major West Coast cities. Check it out at www.jetsuitex.com.

Political Advocacy & Engagement

She Should Run: This organization is dedicated to dramatically increasing the number of women in public leadership by eliminating barriers to success. Sheshouldrun.org.

African American Mayors Association: Because being the mayor of a city or town is downright sexy. Ourmayors.org.

Emily's List: A political action committee that aims to help elect female candidates to office. emilyslist.org.

Article: "Michelle Obama's 'Becoming' is the best-selling hardcover book of the year" (Top book of the whole year! How awesome is that?) https://wapo.st/2DcD3TW.

Register to Vote: And then encourage five of your friends to register too at usa.gov/register-to-vote.

Black Women in Politics: An online list of women who are running. Updated regularly. You can click on people's names to find out what their stances and beliefs are at blackwomeninpolitics.com.

GETTING TO YOUR NEXT LEVEL:

A Prompting Journal

What are your superpowers?

_____

_____

_____

_____

_____

_____

_____

_____

_____

_____

_____

_____

_____

_____

_____

_____

How can you leverage those powers to get to the next level?

_____

_____

_____

_____

_____

_____

_____

_____

_____

_____

_____

_____

_____

_____

_____

_____

_____

What are your goals for your near future?

_____

_____

_____

_____

_____

_____

_____

_____

_____

_____

_____

_____

_____

_____

_____

_____

What's over the horizon for you? What are some goals for the rest of your life?

_____

_____

_____

_____

_____

_____

_____

_____

_____

_____

_____

_____

_____

_____

_____

What are the steps for getting there?

_____

_____

_____

_____

_____

_____

_____

_____

_____

_____

_____

_____

_____

_____

_____

_____

Who are your friends and mentors who can help you get there?

_____

_____

_____

_____

_____

_____

_____

_____

_____

_____

_____

_____

_____

_____

_____

_____

Who are the people YOU can mentor?

_____

_____

_____

_____

_____

_____

_____

_____

_____

_____

_____

_____

_____

_____

What's your story?

_____

_____

_____

_____

_____

_____

_____

_____

_____

_____

_____

_____

_____

_____

_____

Do you want to change your story?

_____

_____

_____

_____

_____

_____

_____

_____

_____

_____

_____

_____

_____

_____

_____

_____

In one line, what is the best answer to the question "Who are you?"

_____

_____

_____

_____

_____

_____

In one line, what is the best answer to the question, "What do you do?"

_____

_____

_____

_____

_____

_____

What's your financial story?

_____

_____

_____

_____

_____

_____

_____

_____

_____

_____

_____

_____

_____

How can you attract more money into your life?

_____

_____

_____

_____

_____

_____

_____

_____

_____

_____

_____

_____

_____

_____

What does "keeping it real" mean to you?

_____

_____

_____

_____

_____

_____

_____

_____

_____

_____

_____

_____

_____

_____

_____

_____

Are you keeping it real?

_____

_____

_____

_____

_____

_____

_____

_____

_____

_____

_____

_____

_____

_____

_____

_____

What do you want to contribute to the world?

_____

_____

_____

_____

_____

_____

_____

_____

_____

_____

_____

_____

_____

_____

_____

_____

_____

What difference can you make in the world; how can you give back?

_____

_____

_____

_____

_____

_____

_____

_____

_____

_____

_____

_____

_____

_____

_____

_____

How can you shine your light more and be the star you are?

_____

_____

_____

_____

_____

_____

_____

_____

_____

_____

_____

_____

_____

_____

_____

What is your strategy to level up?

_____

_____

_____

_____

_____

_____

_____

_____

_____

_____

_____

_____

_____

_____

_____

_____

ABOUT THE AUTHOR

Karen Arrington is the founder of the Miss Black USA Pageant. More than a pageant, it's a movement— celebrating the talents and achievements of today's black women and awarding college scholarships every year.

Since founding the pageant in 1986, Karen has mentored over a thousand young women, helping them get into top medical schools, land major modeling and recording contracts, secure life-changing grants and sponsorship deals, and more.

In addition to running the pageant, Karen is a philanthropist and humanitarian whose work has touched millions of lives. She's the cofounder of Diabetes Awareness Day in West Africa and was named a goodwill ambassador to The Gambia and to the Republic of Sierra Leone.

Karen has received numerous awards including leadership awards from The Lifetime Network and Jones New York and the Trailblazer's Award from the Zeta Phi Sorority (the highest award that is bestowed in this sorority which has over twenty-one thousand members). She has also received honors from Maryland Black Mayors Inc. for commitment and dedication to the community and was a *Woman's Day* magazine Red Dress Honoree along with CNN's Sanjay Gupta and Olympic gold medalist Dana Vollmer. Karen has been interviewed in places like *The Washington Post, Woman's Day, Jet,* and on *BET*.

More info about Karen's work can be found at karenarrington.com and missblackusa.org.

the tiny press

An imprint of Mango Publishing

At The Tiny Press, we believe that small actions—and small books—can create a big ripple effect in our world.

Our mission is to create short books (around 100 pages) that are inspiring, uplifting, and encouraging.

We know you have lots of priorities in your life—work, family, errands, and more. Sometimes it can feel like there's "*just no time left*" to curl up with a book. We hope Tiny Press can provide a happy solution by offering "tiny" books—books that make sense for busy people with full, demanding lives.

With each book, our goal is to make your day a little better than it was before.

Founded in 2018 by Alexandra Franzen (alexandrafranzen.com) in collaboration with Mango Publishing (mango.bz).

Find more Tiny Press books on the Mango website, on Amazon, and everywhere books are sold.